SMART WOMEN AT WORK

12 Steps to Career Breakthroughs

SMART WOMEN AT WORK

12 Steps to Career Breakthroughs

TERRY WARD

CONTEMPORARY
BOOKS, INC.
CHICAGO • NEW YORK

Published by Contemporary Books, Inc.
180 North Michigan Avenue, Chicago, Illinois 60601
Manufactured in the United States of America
International Standard Book Number: 0-8092-4681-3

Published simultaneously in Canada by Beaverbooks, Ltd.
195 Allstate Parkway, Valleywood Business Park
Markham, Ontario L3R 4T8 Canada

Special thanks go
to my husband, Gary,
who loves and supports
me in everything I do.
He is my endless
resource and mentor.
Also, I am grateful
to our own set
of smart women,
Greta, Hilary, and Ingrid.

CONTENTS

SPECIAL THANKS

To Margaret and Ward Tucker
who gave me the confidence
on which I still rely.

SMART WOMEN AT WORK

12 Steps to Career Breakthroughs

INTRODUCTION

You, too, can join women all over America who are working intelligently and getting ahead in their careers. Management has long since realized employees with high levels of personal ambition do well for their companies and for themselves. Personal success does not preclude excellence in service to one's employer. Moreover, individuals who are motivated to upgrade their pay scale and job status make the most desirable employees. In short, they hustle.

Don't be embarrassed or apologetic if you want to get ahead. On the contrary, be embarrassed if you don't. But remember, getting ahead can't happen by wishing. What you do at work today affects your success for tomorrow. If you are engaging in questionable work habits, you're holding yourself back. Perhaps you think you deserve bad habits since something about your work displeases you. The reality you must face is negative behavior invariably makes things more displeasing, at which point you may rationalize another bad habit, and from there you keep going downhill and defeating yourself.

However, if you are making a conscientious effort toward developing productive work habits, you will experience success. A systematic effort toward training yourself in positive behaviors and attitudes at work is the key. Picture what you know about building an elegantly designed house complete with beautiful landscaping. If the house is to turn out as lovely as imagined, every step in building must be executed properly; no step may be skipped. We've all seen hundreds of unattractive houses which stand for decades with no character or charm whatsoever. Your job will probably stand the same way, but is mediocrity all you want? Think again of building a stunning house. Apply the same step-by-step building principles to your work, and you may very well find yourself with a stunning career. You will absolutely find out about the huge difference between feeling successful and feeling stagnant at work.

The following characteristics are constants in the careers of all women who are getting ahead:

- An abundance of energy and initiative.

- A determination to do things right.

- An understanding of the way their particular work fits into the major goals of their companies.

- A level of interest that stays vibrant over the years.

- A cooperative spirit and teamwork advocacy with male and female colleagues.

Make these key concepts a regular part of your work life and you will enjoy your own brand of success. You'll be among the most quietly effective and powerful group of people in America today.

Myths and Realities

(and the benefits of knowing the difference)

MYTH NUMBER ONE

Getting ahead means becoming president of a company and earning six figures.

A WOMAN AT WORK

"If I can sell clothes in a department store for ten years, I know I can sell clothes in a shop of my own."

This is what Jayne Centerfield told herself at age fifty when she started preparing to open her new shop. Was she looking to make megabucks? No, she was looking to run an outstanding shop with a style all its own. Was she trying to become a queen bee boss? No, she was interested mainly in managing herself well enough to work productively with employees as well as handle all the other aspects of running a business. With these general goals in mind, Jayne spent a year doing research, identified short and long range goals, and put together a sound business plan to acquire financing.

This preliminary work gave her a big dose of experience in self-management before the shop ever served its first customer. It wasn't easy all the time, but Jayne refused to lose heart. By the time she finally opened to the public, Jayne had already experienced a special and personal brand of success as a business woman. Somehow, she had found the self-discipline to pull together all the necessary details to open her store properly.

From day one, the shop reflected all the creative touches and stylishness Jayne had visualized in her mind. Old customer relationships built over the years in her department store job served as a beginning base of customers for the new shop, and Jayne was off to a terrific start. Ironically, she did end up in the six figure and big boss category (three stores and 46 employees later), but not because she sought those things to the exclusion of everything else. Jayne insists that she made it, and is still in the process of making it, because she always focused on her two original goals; developing above-average shops and adhering to a strict code of professionalism.

MYTH NUMBER ONE
Getting ahead means becoming president of a company and earning six figures.

REALITY

The business of getting ahead is not an all or nothing proposition. It can be more accurately described as any improvement in pay, title, responsibility, and/or working conditions. These improvements usually come in the form of small steps forward that go unnoticed by others. But take heart, for these seemingly insignificant steps can lead to major breakthroughs. Don't underestimate the importance of any move toward getting ahead. You probably have many to your credit already.

• Be proud of them.

• Be thankful for them.

• Be ever on the alert for opportunities to add to them.

21

BENEFITS OF DISPELLING THE MYTH

Debunking the myth that getting ahead means becoming president of a company and earning six figures reveals the following valuable truths:

- Personal success at work must be defined in terms of goals reached. Therefore, if you have no goals, you can have no success.

- Goals may be conceived in hopes and dreams, but to be of value, goals must ultimately be clearly defined and reachable.

- Success is different things to different people.

To determine your personal definition of career success, you must examine your goals. Therefore, your most important present goal should go something like this:

> "I am going to have three short range goals and three long range goals formulated and written down within the next two weeks. I will accomplish this by thinking carefully about what I want from my career, by collecting information on what is available to me, and by selecting goals well within my reach in order to give myself a chance to experience success."

EXAMPLES OF SHORT RANGE GOALS

1. By next month, put together a one page resume that is formal, polished, and professional. (There are dozens of resources to help you with this. Check the library.)

2. Start a journal entitled, *Personal Work Experience and*

Training. Each week for six months write cryptic notes about your work life. Include job responsibilities, involvement in training programs, progress toward reaching your goals, and personal observations on what has and has not helped you move forward. Be sure to date each entry.

3. Set a date to review and evaluate your journal notes before continuing them. Can you see how useful a journal could be in helping you organize and document your work experience? Can you also see what a valuable tool it could become as you prepare to meet long range goals?

EXAMPLES OF LONG RANGE GOALS

1. Receive a substantial raise this year. Here's where the documented information in your journal could prove invaluable as you organize reasons why you deserve a raise. You can't ask for a raise and expect to get it if you can't communicate in a positive and professional way why you deserve it. A clear and specific statement of what you've done and what you plan to do will get far more attention than whining about needing more money, or, worse than that, making edgy demands for a bigger paycheck.

2. By this time next year, seek consideration for a higher level job than you have now. The same common sense applies in this situation that applies in asking for a raise. First, a cultivation process must be developed. The rapport you establish with your colleagues, the people who work under you, and your superiors sets the stage for them to think of you as advancement material. You can't

seriously expect to be considered for upper level jobs if you skip the process of building mutual respect with people above and below you.

3. Be funded in next year's budget to take part in a work-related out of town conference or training session. Again, requests of this magnitude require setting up over a period of time. If you spot a conference you'd like to attend, make sure it's dated far enough in the future to allow for planning and budgeting on the part of your boss, and make double sure you can articulate how the information you intend to bring back is going to make your department and boss look good.

NOTE: The examples of written goals outlined above were designed to help you formulate written goals of your own. You may have many different goals than the ones mentioned. As you hammer out personal goals, make sure you have a specific time frame surrounding each one. Also keep in mind that short range goals are easier to manage. Long range goals can also be reached with great success, but they require more persistence.

EXAMPLE: Jenna decided she wanted to change jobs within two years. Her secretarial position in a printing company had provided her much experience, but she felt a job in sales would allow her to make more money and develop a wider range of skills. Jenna put her goal in writing and then set up a two pronged effort toward reaching it. First, she tried to make herself a model employee in her current job. Second, she set about establishing a professional relationship with all the sales people who called on her boss at the printing company. It took six months longer than she planned, but Jenna finally landed a sales job she found out about through one of her newly cultivated contacts. Selling office supplies became Jenna's new job responsibility, and her former employer became her first and best customer. Jenna feels no less successful that her job change took six months longer than she anticipated, but she does admit she might have pulled if off sooner had she approached it a bit more systematically. Jenna realizes, as should you and I, that although creative strategies and goals for getting ahead are limitless, we must tap into them persistently and systematically if they are to do us any good. The following quote speaks eloquently about the value of persistence. Make it a KEY POINTER in planning your career.

> "Press on: Nothing in the world can take the place of persistence. Talent will not; nothing is more common than unsuccessful individuals with talent. Genius will not; unrewarded genius is almost a proverb. Education will not; the world is full of educated derelicts. Persistence and determination alone are omnipotent."

STRATEGIES FOR BROADENING YOUR CAREER HORIZON

1. Go forward with a *Personal Work Experience and Training Journal* as described on page 22. Reserve a section in the back of your journal and label it, "GOALS." Be sure to date all entries in your journal, including goals. Do not overload the goals section or you will defeat yourself. Better to check off completed goals than to struggle with unrealistic goals you can't meet. To save time, make your weekly entries thoughtful but short. If you keep a note-

book of this type for six months, you will establish in your own mind that you do, indeed, intend to get ahead. You will experience the gratification of translating vague wishes and dreams into organized, written goals.

Maintaining a journal for six months will also give you insight into yourself. You may see patterns emerge which will cue you to take a career direction that never occurred to you before. You may even find yourself doing something constructive just to have the pleasure of recording it in your journal. And you absolutely will benefit from practice in setting and meeting goals.

2. Start a campaign of getting to know people all over your company or agency (and other companies when you get a chance), and make a special effort to become pleasantly acquainted with people in jobs above your level. If you present yourself as a courteous, friendly, and well groomed person who doesn't mind introducing herself, you will be hard to resist and even harder to forget. Throw in a carefully built reputation for working hard and producing results, and your credibility factor will soar. Remember, moves forward (and backward) occur because of decisions made by people. Obviously then, you would benefit from getting to know a great many worthwhile people in your field. You can do it; just stick out your hand and say "hello."

THOUGHT QUESTIONS TO PROBE YOUR MIND

1. Can you give two positive examples of goal-oriented behavior at work?

2. How would you describe the condition of being without goals?

3. From your observation, do you think many of the people you work with have bothered to write down specific, well thought out goals for their work lives?

4. What do the following phrases mean to you?

   "Drawing your breath and drawing your pay."

   "Marking time."

   "Living the same year over and over."

MYTH NUMBER TWO
*Getting ahead means
becoming a workaholic.*

A WOMAN AT WORK

"I've always worked, I've always played tennis, and I've always enjoyed my husband and children. Sure, different things take precedence at different times, but everyone has to do a certain amount of juggling whether she works or not. My secret to handling everything is in setting priorities and planning my time. I know it sounds simplistic, but it works. Granted, a wheel runs off occasionally, but that's to be expected. When it happens, I just pick it up and move on."

Marian Joyner, an energetic branch bank manager, makes her philosophy clear. Work is a big part of her life, but it isn't all there is. With such a cavalier attitude how did she work her way up to branch manager? Simple. She has well developed goals and a good sense of perspective on what is important. She practices excellent time management and depends on her ability to focus intensively on important tasks rather than wasting endless hours on things that don't matter. She is organized and efficient, but has also learned that a sense of humor can carry her through much pressure and many foul-ups. Marian doesn't see herself as very different from other women, and she is generous with encouragement to everyone who works at her branch. Although only thirty-five, her superiors already view her as an up-and-coming employee. Marian is known to be a very professional career woman, as well as a warm and loving family person, and the nicest part about her is her certainty that any woman can be known the same way.

MYTH NUMBER TWO
Getting ahead means becoming a workaholic.

REALITY

A balanced life contributes far more to your advancement than excessive hours at work. A forty hour work week provides enough time to set in motion scores of tactics designed to improve your job situation. You have to spend the time at work anyway, so you may as well make it count for your future. Think of your actual hours at work as having two purposes; working for your employer and working for yourself. Now think of your pay as having two forms; money and experience. Start looking at the time you spend at work as a paid education. Your employer will benefit from having you learn all you can about your job, and you will benefit from broadening your skill and knowledge base. Get in the habit of using your workday to sharpen your skills.

Now let's consider after work activities designed to help you with career development. There are literally hundreds of degrees, books, tapes, manuals, trade journals, lectures, and classes chock-full of information for career people who want to hone their skills. Some after work time needs to be devoted to these learning avenues, but you must be selective. The more intensely you train yourself during working hours to identify useful skills and strategies, the easier it will be to choose appropriate after work career development opportunities. Make your involvement in career training a routine part of your life, but schedule activities outside your home at reasonable intervals.

Reserve a few drawers or shelves in your home for books and other printed materials related specifically to the advancement of your career. It will be gratifying to watch your collection grow over the years. Be cautious, however, of trying to do too much too soon. It's far better to train for success at a pace you can sustain over a lifetime than to race ahead toward exhaustion and burnout.

- Do use your working hours to discover and practice skills for advancement.

- Do seek appropriate training after work.

- Do pace yourself so you can work for a lifetime toward getting ahead.

- Don't neglect your personal life by scheduling all your time for work and training.

- Do be good to yourself by spending time regularly on relaxation, play, or whatever else makes you happy.

- Do understand you are more likely to get ahead if you:

1. Approach it as a manageable system as opposed to an overwhelming impossibility.

2. Activate the process regularly over the whole span of your work life.

3. Pace yourself as you move along by scheduling your time sensibly in all areas of your life.

BENEFITS OF DISPELLING THE MYTH

Debunking the myth that getting ahead means becoming a workaholic eradicates one more excuse for not acting. You can no longer say, "There's no use in my trying to advance because I don't have the energy or time to make it happen." Many women will continue saying and believing this, but not you. You will start using the time you have instead of complaining about the time you don't have. You may not be able to quit your job and work on an advanced degree, but you can use your workday to learn everything possible about your job and the field of work in which you are involved. You may not be able to attend week-long seminar training sessions, but you can enroll in appropriate local classes. The main thing is to use your time wisely and to make the very best of whatever training programs are within your reach. Forget limitations and concentrate on opportunities. Smart women have been doing this for decades.

KEY POINTERS

- Successful people may use their time differently, but they don't have any more of it than you do.

- Successful people may go through periods of working too hard or putting in grueling hours, but they can't sustain it indefinitely any more than you can.

- Successful people have learned to strike time and energy balances in their lives. These same balances are available to you.

- Successful people really believe they deserve to be on a track of advancement, and you must believe the same thing about yourself.

- You deserve to get ahead; now start behaving as though you do.

- Don't believe in magic wishes that take you to a career fantasyland, but don't believe in hopelessness, either.

- You have control.

- Your actions and attitudes make a difference.

- You can get ahead if you want to.

STRATEGIES FOR BROADENING YOUR CAREER HORIZON

1. Think about how your twenty-four hour day breaks down. Most of us spend a third or more of each weekday at our jobs. Ask yourself if you want to let a whole third of your life slip away with no concrete plan for improvement.

2. Now think about how your workday breaks down. As you go through your schedule mentally, jot down a few self advancement opportunities you've been missing. Let the following examples help you get started:

- Reserve a large file folder at work for materials specifically related to career advancement.

- Make a list of women working in positions above your level. If you can't think of any, your employer may have an unwritten understanding about which jobs women can fill, and your career advancement may have to continue elsewhere.

- Observe closely the men and women in positions above

you.

• Dress and carry yourself as well or better than they do, and do it consistently. You have to look and act the part if you expect to get the part.

• Establish yourself as a serious and hard working employee, and then ask your direct superior for advice on how to advance. Only a real brute would discourage you.

• Speak positively every chance you get about your department or work setting. Your boss will be grateful, and you will be viewed as someone who is in an excellent job situation instead of as someone who is downtrodden and miserable.

• Monitor your speech carefully because what you say at work greatly influences how you're viewed at work.

THOUGHT QUESTIONS TO PROBE YOUR MIND

1. Do you really acknowledge the fact that a significant portion of your time and energy is spent in a formal work setting? If you spent the same amount of time playing tennis or golf, do you think you could advance in skill? Are you now open to the idea of applying this line of reasoning to your career life?

2. Have you thought much about the value of time? You wouldn't squander $800.00 a day, or even $8.00 a day. Why then would you squander eight hours a day at work by drifting along instead of plotting your advancement?

MYTH NUMBER THREE
Men have it easy.

A WOMAN AT WORK

"When I started moving through the ranks of college administrative positions, I acquired a different perspective on the accomplishments of men. The work required is just as demanding for men as it is for women. I no longer assume men receive more amenities in the working world just because they are male, nor do I still think women receive less just because they are female. Before passing judgment on the fairness of a person's career situation, I want to know two things: the difficulty of the work, and what the individual, male or female, has done to help himself or herself.

The intense responsibility connected with my own job has caused me to develop a new respect for individuals who held the position before me, and it just so happens all those individuals were men. I think a lot of women at my level are realizing the guys have been working a lot harder all these years than we may have first thought."

Anna Parker spoke another language a decade ago when she was in graduate school. At that time she was very vocal about her belief that men had all the power simply because they were men. She was always on the bandwagon of showing up her male classmates, which she did quite well by being an honor graduate and the recipient of several awards. Her competitive spirit and willingness to work hard ulti-

43

mately lifted her to the high level college administrative job she now holds. The curious thing is that along the way she was forced to overcome many of the same obstacles men have been overcoming for years. She has also felt the pressure of several jobs that were previously for men only. Were these jobs easy? Anna's five word answer sums up her new awareness succinctly. "No, and they *never were*."

MYTH NUMBER THREE
Men have it easy.

REALITY

Nothing could be further from the truth. Men have been slugging it out in the world of work for centuries, and it was never easy. Men have been so busy working they have not had time to raise an outcry against unfair obstacles in the way of their career development. Whether confronting a World War, a Great Depression, or a simple office conflict, men have pressed on stoically in their efforts to make a living. They have not railed against the unjust system that decided their fate. In fact, they have totally embraced society's measure of what is means to be a man. They believe all worthwhile men:

• Work and work hard.

• Compete with other men for the job and the dollar.

- Compete with ever increasing numbers of working women for the same job and dollar.

- Ask no questions as to what they might do with their lives other than work.

- Labor for decades to put food on the table and a degree of financial security in the bank.

- Stand aghast when flatly informed that what men have really been doing all these years is self actualizing and engaging in personal growth and development at the expense of their wives and other women. ("Self actualizing?" echo the fellows. "And all this time we thought we were just trying to make a living.")

- Press on in spite of their newest and most confusing competitors, women.

BENEFITS OF DISPELLING THE MYTH

Debunking the myth that men have it easy can trigger attitude changes which make you ripe for learning and applying techniques needed to get ahead at work. Like it or not, fair or not, men have seniority in the work arena. They've earned it. Now it's your turn to earn it the same way. Watch and learn from successful men (and women, too, of course). Read voraciously about the ones you don't know personally. Observe the ones you do know and notice the smallest details of how they operate. Ask them questions about how they started. You'll find most of them came from humble beginnings in their careers and had to work up through many menial jobs. You'll also learn volumes about their tenacity, perseverance, and strong beliefs in themselves.

Was it easy for them to become successful? A resounding no.

Has it become easier as their successes built up over the years? Perhaps a bit, but it certainly was never the snap you might have expected or wished it to be.

Was it worth the effort? A resounding yes.

KEY POINTER

You have the privilege and opportunity to choose your male and female work models. Select those of the highest caliber and think consciously about their work styles. Emulate as many of their finer work habits and attitudes as you can, and you will see unmistakable evidence of progress in your work life. The wisdom of this strategy is very useful, but it's entirely up to you to claim it.

STRATEGIES FOR BROADENING
YOUR CAREER HORIZON

1. Think broadly about work. There is a context within which we all operate which can be described as follows: Men and women as groups are at different levels developmentally in the world of work. Don't think of this in terms of bad or good; think of it in terms of what is real. You will make better decisions if you make them based on reality.

2. Cooperate with men at work; don't fight them. They control plenty and have the power to help or hinder you.

3. Approach people as individuals and be sensitive to their perspectives. For example, if an older man calls you Honey or Sweetheart in a business setting, don't be offended and don't make an issue of it. Understand that he probably means no disrespect and may very well be trying to express approval.

4. Help people save face. If you do things to help associates feel good about themselves, you make business friends. The simple courtesy of remembering a person's name is a good example. People find it hard to forget an individual who makes them feel good.

5. Keep your guard up. Be on the alert for hidden agenda and learn to read people and situations on deeper than surface levels. The beast called "office politics" thrives on what is going on beneath the surface, but he isn't deadly if you stay alert to the fact that people very often have hidden motives. Moreover, as you practice being perceptive about the intricacies of relationships, you'll find you can learn as much from subtleties of behaviors and attitudes as you

can from what people say and do at surface levels.

6. Never underestimate people. You don't have the market cornered on figuring things out. People may not say it to your face, but they know if you try to use, manipulate, or undermine them. They also see through bragging, shallow attempts at acting superior, and name dropping. If you can see positives and negatives in others, be assured they can see them in you.

7. Concentrate on your individual effort toward getting ahead rather than depending on women as a group to help you. If you make breakthroughs for yourself, you'll pave the way for other women to do the same. Remember, any successful group is made up of individuals who realize they must help themselves before they can help others. Approach your advancement as an individual, not as a crusader for a cause. Women who excel individually lend a degree of credibility to all women. Be that kind of woman and you will enjoy the power and satisfaction of being able to help others.

THOUGHT QUESTIONS TO PROBE YOUR MIND

1. There are hundreds of positives for being a woman in today's work force. Can you name three?

2. Admit to yourself at least two ways you've taken advantage of being a woman on the job. (Come on now. We're all guilty of this one.)

3. Have you ever criticized men as a group for the way they treat women at work? If so, have you stopped to think about your grievances in an historical context or from the male point of view? Do you really, sincerely, honestly believe that men are the enemy?

MYTH NUMBER FOUR
Successful men and women
are smarter than you.

A WOMAN AT WORK

"I made better grades in college and law school than many of my male classmates, but that doesn't mean I can compete with them in the real world. They know so much more than I do about inspiring confidence in clients. Sometimes I think they were just born with that ability. I know for certain that making clients feel secure is what it takes to build a thriving practice, but I'm not sure I can pull it off."

Amelia Canfield testifies by word and deed that she believes her male colleagues are brighter. The sad thing is the men haven't tried to intimidate her at all. They don't need to because Amelia intimidates herself. The job she holds as attorney for a private women's college has become a hiding place, almost a prison. Amelia has outgrown her job, but she's afraid to break out and do what she originally planned which was to start a law practice of her own. She is terrified of failing, so she won't allow herself to pursue her dream. It's interesting to hear Amelia relate story after story of the ups and downs experienced by her friends in private practice. Some of the downs she describes are fairly rugged, but she always maintains that her friends can handle them. Why can't she give herself the same credit?

MYTH NUMBER FOUR
Successful men and women are smarter than you.

REALITY

You are just as intelligent and capable as your fellow human beings. They are not smarter than you. In point of fact, the process of learning and applying strategies for getting ahead doesn't require a superhuman intellect anyway. Be advised now and forevermore that you have ample brain power to think up hundreds of creative ideas to help yourself get ahead. The suggestions and encouragement offered on these pages are meant to help you in tangible and specific ways, but they are also designed to make you aware of your own responsibility. You must not only practice applying these suggestions, you must also get in the habit of continually devising new ones. If you're uncertain about whether or not you're able to help yourself get ahead, consider what you've already accomplished. Mustering the self discipline to get up and go to work at any job everyday for even six months is significant. You've done that and much more, so stop selling yourself short and take hold of the notion that you can get ahead because of your own initiative.

BENEFITS OF DISPELLING THE MYTH

Debunking the myth that successful men and women are smarter than you is of paramount importance. It breaks down a tremendous barrier between you and advancement. It also allows you to confidently explore the following thought processes:

- Facing the fact that there is no mystique or magic about getting ahead.

- Forsaking any secret wish you may be harboring that there are short cuts, easy routes, or simplistic formulas for advancement.

- Giving up the idea that lightning will strike and catapult you ahead.

KEY POINTER

You have a perfectly adequate brain. Trust it as your very best resource in developing personal strategies for advancing in your career.

STRATEGIES FOR BROADENING YOUR CAREER HORIZON

1. Practice thinking of yourself as a very smart and capable individual. I once saw a bank president lock his keys inside his car. After twenty minutes of struggling, he managed to open the car door with a coat hanger, but not without shredding the rubber window insulation. Two hours later the same man locked the same keys in his trunk.

This time he had to call a locksmith to pick the lock for a fee of $25. Clearly, this bank president isn't smarter than you. He may be older, more experienced, or more intimidating, but he is not smarter. Remember this story the next time you come across people you think are successful and brainy. Your head is just as good as theirs.

2. Abide by the following LAWS to insure that others perceive you as the intelligent person you are:

    L ook sharp.

    A ct sharp.

    W rite sharp.

    S peak sharp.

3. Align yourself with the most responsible and serious minded people you can find in your work setting. You know precisely which ones are respected and which ones are viewed as lazy and incompetent. Cultivate the former; keep your distance from the latter.

4. Be so smart that you know when to be ignorant. The ability to keep your mouth shut about sensitive issues is practically considered a spiritual virtue by employers. After all, is it really necessary to talk about the argument you overheard your boss having with her spouse on the phone? When pumped for sensitive information by others, resist the temptation to be "in the know." It is very valuable to be considered an information resource, but restrict the information you give out to professional matters.

5. Have the wisdom to recognize situations that can work to your advantage. The psychological balancing act in work relationships can often tip the scales in your favor.

For instance, if you have a scheduled appointment with someone and they forget about it or show up late, you will have a psychological advantage the next time you see that person. You may even discover a willingness on their part to do something extra for you to even the score. Be ready to guide this person toward a favor you want. Men have been cashing in chips with each other for years, but you can "cash in" as well as they can. If you really want things like raises and promotions, keep track of your psychological "chips," but do it gracefully, subtly, and fairly.

6. Become smarter by reading about your area of work on a regular basis. Since most people don't bother to read very much or think very deeply, this one strategy has the potential to lift you head and shoulders above your colleagues. READ!

THOUGHT QUESTIONS TO PROBE YOUR MIND

1. Have you ever played the "if only" game? It goes like this:
If only I were smarter or richer or better looking or better educated, I might be able to get further ahead at work.
If only I were as bright as the people I see sailing through
their careers, maybe I could do better for myself. Will you
be able to recognize yourself or others playing the "if only" game the next time you come across it? How do you
intend to cure yourself of indulging in these kinds of self
defeating activities?

2. Do you treat yourself gently or harshly when you make
mistakes? It's normal to be cautious for a while after a
botch-up, but do you become immobilized? Have you
figured out that most people are too busy with their own
lives to concern themselves with your shortcomings? Do
you really believe the old axiom, "You learn more from
failure than from success?" Can you remember to be kind
to yourself the next twelve times you miss the mark? If
you can, you'll be joining a prestigious group of people
who manage to go forward inspite of, as well as because
of, their hundreds of mistakes and failures.

3. Are you open to new ideas and change, or are you more
comfortable following the same patterns year after year?
Fear of change can raise many emotion-packed questions
in your psyche:

   • Will I have to work longer hours?

   • Will I have to learn something new?

   • Am I capable of learning something new?

   • Will I have to give up anything?

- Am I losing ground or gaining ground?

- Will it be too much work?

- Why can't I just do what I'm accustomed to?

4. Which of the above questions creeps into your mind? Can you see that if you rigidly hang onto status quo and refuse to flow with change, you will become hopelessly outdated? Can you describe what it means to be a living anachronism?

MYTH NUMBER FIVE

Assertiveness yields power. It is responsible for a new thrust of progress among women striving to advance at work.

A WOMAN AT WORK

"I never said anything that wasn't perfectly true or fair. In fact, my willingness to articulate what is right is the main reason I was hired in the first place. Too bad it had to be my undoing, too."

Barbara Marshall still hasn't figured out why she was fired from her job as lobbyist for a well known professional association. Even as she tells her story, it's clear from her tone and choice of words that she believes fairness has been totally violated. Barbara is convinced a co-worker filtered information to her boss that Barbara was losing effectiveness on behalf of the association due to repeated incidents of abrasiveness in committee meetings. Barbara, however, believes she did nothing more than stand up for what was right. It has been only recently that she began to suspect her style may have been too strong, aggressive, and perhaps even too argumentative. She now concedes her efforts were unsuccessful because she alienated more people than she befriended. Barbara is learning the confusing lesson that being right isn't always enough in the working world. You not only have to be right, you have to be tactfully right.

MYTH NUMBER FIVE
Assertiveness yields power. It is responsible for a new thrust of progress among women striving to advance at work.

REALITY

"Assertiveness" has become a fashionable word, a buzz word, a word which holds out false hope to women by suggesting that if only they can become "assertive," they can gain enough power to get ahead. By one definition *assert* means, "to state positively; affirm; aver." It also means, "to maintain as a right or claim, by words or by force." Some women have used a shrill tone in documenting the "rights and claims" of women. Basically, they've issued two lists: *Things We Should Not Tolerate,* and *Things We Should Demand.* It is time to compile a third list labeled, *Things We Should Learn About: Professionalism, Cooperation, Getting*

Along, and Contribution. Successful people have always focused on the positive and minimized the negative, and so must you if you want to move ahead.

BENEFITS OF DISPELLING THE MYTH

Debunking the myth that assertiveness yields power will help you think more clearly about good and bad advice on career advancement. No issue is cut and dried, and that includes the question of assertiveness. Evaluating assertiveness training in terms of the following guidelines will also help you appraise other career related advice as it applies to you personally:

Point — Beware assertiveness if it becomes a veiled excuse for:

• Abrasiveness

• Aggression

• Complaining

• Rudeness

• Clamoring to be understood

• Airing resentments

• Putting down others

Point — Embrace assertiveness if it means finding the courage to affirm the following positives:

• Sharpening your technical capabilities.

• Learning and practicing people skills.

• Improving your attitude.

• Setting and achieving realistic goals.

• Being on the lookout for all opportunities to enhance your value to your employer.

• Declaring confidently to yourself and others that you are working to get ahead and are trying to learn and activate all positive and reasonable strategies to that end.

KEY POINTERS

Assertiveness in the form of bemoaning unfairness, making demands, and attempting to negotiate on trivial matters will not endear you to your employer. Whether or not this is fair is beside the point; we are addressing what is real, not what is fair.

Assertiveness in the form of steadiness, poise, and a positive attitude is a valued and rare trait. Couple this positive form of assertiveness with a willingness to do your official job plus a little more, and you will set yourself apart. You will have an edge. You will, indeed, have power. It may mean training yourself to wait a week before expressing what you think about someone or something that has made you angry. It may mean withstanding subtle, and not so subtle, pressure from fellow employees who would rather see you remain on their level of mediocrity. It may mean being clever enough to maintain positive relationships with your peers, subordinates, and bosses, at the same time you're actively advancing your own cause. You will not succeed in every situation, but don't worry about that. Instead, dwell on the large and small successes that spring from consistent effort. Say to yourself everyday.

"I am steady and poised."

"I have a positive attitude."

"I am known to be a hard worker which helps my employer

as much as it helps me."

"I am recognized as being serious about my work."

"My co-workers know I enjoy my work."

If you repeat the suggested phrases and act them out, things will start falling into place. When you get discouraged, pick up this book and review the basics. Then encourage yourself to go forward positively. You deserve to get ahead. You are able to get ahead. You will get ahead if you train your mind to expect it. Practice the positive kind of assertiveness that will help you hang onto your desire, and you will be giving yourself something no one else can give you. Yes, there's room for being assertive in your quest for career advancement, but only in exceedingly positive manifestations.

STRATEGIES TO BROADEN
YOUR CAREER HORIZON

1. Listen with a third ear to trendy words and phrases such as assertiveness, productivity, networking, stress management, time management, management by objectives, and "1" minute anything. These are just a few terms suffering from overkill. The ideas behind them contain gems of wisdom, but the words themselves are bandied about by many people who are often guilty of talking the talk without walking the walk. Keep yourself out of that category.

2. Learn the meanings of these words:

   Discern — ". . .to distinguish mentally; recognize as distinct or different."

Discriminate — "...to note or observe a difference; distinguish accurately."

EXAMPLE: A life insurance plan featuring very low premiums was presented to a group of employees. It was an excellent offering made possible because the insurance company also handled the group's health insurance. The employees were winning in two ways; health insurance premiums were being paid by the employer, and inexpensive life insurance policies were being made available as options for group members. It was a genuinely good deal, but only four of fifty-five employees signed up for the life insurance program. The other fifty-four were suffering from jaded notions about deals having to do with money. They thought like this: Since most money deals work out poorly, I should reject all money deals. The four employees who bought the insurance were much more discerning and discriminating thinkers. They applied the following logic: If I categorically reject all money deals, I will miss the good ones along with the bad.

Go back and review the meanings of discern and discriminate. Now you can begin looking for opportunities at work to activate your own discerning and discriminating mind.

3. Develop a mental junk detector for ideas. As you filter information through your "detector," trash will be discarded and valuables will be saved. Just be sure you put good information to use when you find it. For instance, it doesn't do you any good to know how to build a business correspondence network if you refuse to discipline yourself to find time for letter writing.

EXAMPLE: You conceive the notion of starting an annotated index card file of pertinent people you meet during the course of each workday.

- Possible Outcome Number One: You start the file and maintain it for a month or two before letting it go by the wayside.

- Possible Outcome Number Two: You start the file, maintain it for a year, and make an effort to stay in touch with the people in it by sending them Christmas cards, personal notes, and interesting clippings and articles. Then you decide to open your own secretarial service across town, or look for a better job, or market an original newsletter. Your card file could easily provide a base of clients which would propel you on your way to success.

Now do you see the importance of not letting valuable ideas slip away with worthless information? A recent study by Burke Marketing Research, Incorporated, yielded some very useful information for employees who want to be viewed positively. As you review the article which describes the study, try to put yourself in your boss's shoes in order to analyze how your work habits and behaviors are perceived. Empathy for others and a bit of introspection can help you monitor your behavior, make better decisions, and establish improved work habits.

RESULTS OF STUDY REPORTED

Liars, goof-offs, egomaniacs, laggards, rebels, whiners, airheads and sloths — these are the eight banes of a boss's existence, according to a new survey, and each is advised to repent or risk unemployment.

Burke Marketing Research, Inc. asked executives in 100 of the nation's 1,000 largest companies, "What employee behaviors disturb you most?"

The result was a "hit parade of things that stick in the boss's craw — the kind of behavior that hits a nerve," said Marc Silbert whose temporary personnel agency commissioned the survey. "They can blind employers to employees' good qualities. They become beyond redemption."

1. Dishonesty and lying topped the list. "If a company believes that an employee lacks integrity, all positive qualities — ranging from skill and experience to productivity and intelligence — become meaningless," said Silbert, vice president of Accountemps.

"This isn't just the guy who steals money from petty cash," he explained. "It includes intellectual dishonesty. We had one employer complain about an employee who took on a job with a Nov. 16 deadline even though he knew he'd be on vacation that week."

The seven other deadly sins, in order of irritation:

2. Irresponsibility, goofing-off, and doing personal business on company time. "We found some people literally conducting their own ongoing businesses on company time," Silbert said. "It's not just a guy getting a phone call from his wife to pick up eggs on the way home. This is someone running a T-shirt business out of the office. It's entrepreneurial behavior gone wild in a very real way."

3. Arrogance, ego problems, and excessive aggressiveness. "Employees who spend more time boasting about their accomplishments than on actually getting the job done. . .who think that being loud or boisterous will have a positive effect bother their bosses," Silbert said. "If you have this kind of person in a supervisory role, you don't have one problem, you have twenty. You have little range wars breaking out all over the office."

4. Absenteeism and lateness. "One employer said, 'It doesn't make any difference when we start, 9 a.m. or 10 a.m., some people will be 15 minutes late,'" Silbert reported.

5. Not following instructions or ignoring company policies. "Such behavior is more serious in larger, more conservative companies," Silbert said, citing, "a guy working for a dark-suit-and-school-tie kind of company who wears an I'm-from-Florida tie."

6. Whining and complaining. "There's one in every office. They always have a problem: 'Do we have to do it by Thursday?' 'This project is so boring,'" Silbert whined in imitation.

7. Absence of commitment, concern, or dedication. "This often is grounds for absence of raises and promotions," Silbert said.

8. Laziness and lack of motivation. "Both demonstrate that these people don't care about the company, so why should the company care about them," Silbert pointed out.

Among the also-rans: lack of character, inability to get along with others, disrespect, displays of anger or pettiness, making ill-informed decisions and judgments, and taking credit for the work of others.

After studying the preceding article, try to put yourself in your boss's shoes in order to analyze how your own habits and behaviors are perceived. Empathy for others and a bit of introspection can help you monitor your behavior, make better decisions, and establish improved work habits.

THOUGHT QUESTIONS TO PROBE YOUR MIND

1. Have you considered the notion that a back to basics approach to work habits does not have to be in conflict with learning and using new ideas and techniques? Have you identified a personal set of fundamental work habits?

2. Why do you think it is valid to make a case that new work related ideas are not worth much if they ignore or deny the basics?

3. Name one woman you view as having what it takes to get ahead. In your opinion is she attentive to the basics? Does she keep abreast of new ideas? How well does she integrate the two?

4. How do you think your boss and colleagues would describe you in terms of question number three?

MYTH NUMBER SIX

Men must develop their careers; women still have a choice.

A WOMAN AT WORK

"I have come to the conclusion that it isn't fair for me to expect a man to give me the kind of security I want. Oh yes, I'm married, but my husband and I are both developing careers of our own. He expresses a great deal of gratitude for my desire to make significant financial contributions to our family, but the truth is he doesn't have to. I'm doing it for myself as much as for him and the children. He also tells me sad stories about his male friends who suffer terrible guilt over the fact that their wives are forced to work to make ends meet for their families. My question is what would these long suffering women do if they had no man to pick up the major portion of the tab? How can they be so insensitive as to play the role of martyr with their husbands and ignore the millions of single women who have no choice but to make their own way? My theory is that every woman ought to make her own way, and I intend to do just that."

Meg Connelly has no qualms about injecting an element of reality into any conversation about women and careers. Moreover, she presents an excellent model in that she has worked successfully in two fields while managing family life, too. Meg taught school several years and then moved into a bottom rung editor's job in a medium sized publishing company. After several years of experience and interim promotions, she has reached the position of senior editor in charge of manuscript acquisition. One of her ongoing concerns is for women who are just entering the work force. Meg takes every opportunity to encourage them and build up their confidence. "I'm a fan of any working woman," she states emphatically, "no matter what her creed, color, or age, and no matter what her job."

MYTH NUMBER SIX
Men must develop their careers; women still have a choice.

REALITY

Women absolutely need to develop their careers if they aspire to enjoy real security and fulfillment. Now that we have faced the economic reality of having to work, we must go to the next step of advancing as far as we can. Smart women are accepting the challenge. They are finding creative ways to get beyond phase one. They are taking the responsibility of helping themselves and are no longer waiting for husbands, employers, or the women's movement to save them.

BENEFITS OF DISPELLING THE MYTH

Debunking the myth that men must develop their careers and women still have a choice can make you aware of an irreversible trend. There is a great awakening among thinking women on what getting ahead really means. These women find the notion of controlling their own advancement refreshing, and they find the long list of benefits resulting from the effort inspiring.

BENEFITS OF MAKING THE EFFORT

• Being in the mainstream with forward thinking people.

• Realizing that getting ahead results from hundreds of small accomplishments over the years.

• Learning to value every success no matter how small.

• Learning how to take care of yourself and knowing that if you do, you are better able to help others.

• Becoming more valuable to yourself and others.

• Enjoying the fact that you are building your own security.

• Finding the kind of fulfillment which frees you from living vicariously through others.

• Eliminating from your future many of the problems unprepared women will face. For you there will be no:

  1. Empty nest syndrome. (You will be too busy developing your career.)

  2. Financially disastrous widowhood. (Widowhood is never easy emotionally, but at least you will have the comfort of knowing you can provide for yourself.)

3. Financially disastrous divorce. (You will be able to recover faster with the backup of a serious career.)

KEY POINTERS

The first step in getting ahead in your career is realizing you owe it to yourself to try. Other women are not only trying, they are making respectable headway. You, too, must go forward or risk being left behind to be controlled by others. We have put away one set of debilitating laments. Let's check them off one by one and leave them behind forever.

✔ • No one told me I was going to have to work indefinitely for a living.

✔ • My family and society didn't prepare me for a lifetime of work.

✔ • I resent having to work when I planned to stay at home and be a proper wife and mother.

Now it's time to put away another set of laments. Let's check them off, too.

✔ • I know I have to work for a living, but I don't have to spend more than the minimal amount of time and energy on my job, and I certainly don't have to like it.

✔ • My job is not my real life. I just work to get to the end of the day and the beginning of the next paycheck.

✔ • I believe most working women are ill equipped to advance in their careers because they are oppressed by men, not taken seriously, and too overworked at home to even consider trying to get ahead in a career.

It is imperative to expose the above excuses and negative thought patterns if you want to make something special of your career. Many women will continue to hang onto useless and self destructive thought patterns, but not you. You will adhere to the philosophy that work is a grand opportunity, not a distasteful necessity. This positive philosophical stance, plus the belief that you have much personal control over your own progress, will result in work becoming a great source of satisfaction in your life.

STRATEGIES FOR BROADENING YOUR CAREER HORIZON

1. Assume work will be a lifetime proposition, not a temporary inconvenience. Assume you will most likely need to work no matter what else happens in your life.

2. Listen for verbal cues from others that reveal the kind of distorted views listed below:

DISTORTED THINKING	CLEAR THINKING
"I'm just working here until something better comes along."	"Working here is good experience. I'm trying to soak up everything I can."
"When I get married and have children, I'll probably stop working."	"My work life is something I don't plan to give up. The personal security and fulfillment it provides are too precious to sacrifice."
"When my children finish college, I can finally quit working."	"When my children finish college, I plan to go to more conventions, trade shows, and association meetings. It will

"I'm only working to help my husband."

"I had to find a job to get us through a money crisis, but it's strictly temporary."

"It doesn't matter so much if my pay is lower than my husband's. After all, it's only a second income."

"I hate this job, but from what I hear, everybody else hates theirs, too. I guess working is a necessary evil."

"If I had known I was going to be working this long, I would have trained for a better paying job."

be great to have the money to fund more of these growth experiences."

"I'm really working for myself, but my family benefits a great deal from it, too."

"Nothing and nobody forces me to work. I do it because it gives me control over my own fate. Delusions are for others. Getting ahead in my career is for me."

"My career is just as important to me as a man's career is to him. Besides, women are not immune to being cast in the role of chief breadwinner. I'll never minimize the importance of my career."

"I'm too selfish to give up a third of my life to a job I hate, but I also realize it's my responsibility to either adjust my attitude or move on. Nobody is going to fix things for me. I have to fix things for myself."

"I want to be like the exciting men and women I see who are having a great time developing their skills. They always seem to be learning and training and doing exciting things. That's what I want to do, too."

3. Practice telling yourself good things about what you can accomplish and enjoy at work. Repeated affirmations, whether they are positive or negative, make their way into your subconscious mind. This is the part of your brain which can't differentiate between what is vividly imagined and what is real. If you affirm an idea to yourself on a regular basis, your subconscious not only accepts it as fact, it causes you to behave in ways that will make the idea actually become fact. Creating and repeating positive affirmations can be very helpful to you, but it may take a little effort to wade through the negatives your mind has already internalized. If you remember three simple rules, positive affirmations will be of tremendous help to you:

    1. Use present tense.

    2. Say the words with great intensity and emotion.

    3. Speak and act as if the affirmation already exists.

EXAMPLES OF POSITIVE AFFIRMATIONS OF A GENERAL NATURE

- I'm lucky to be alive at a time when opportunities are plentiful for working women.

- I'm proud to see other women making bold efforts to learn and advance.

- I'm glad my personal efforts to do well in my career are opening up more and more opportunities for other women.

NOTE: Positive affirmations like the ones listed above can help you, but specific ones are even more useful.

EXAMPLES OF POSITIVE AFFIRMATIONS
OF A SPECIFIC NATURE

• "I am capable of speaking successfully to a large group."

• "I am able to run my boss's job"

• "I make an excellent impression when being interviewed."

With the listed examples in mind, you can begin creating your own positive affirmations. Just be sure to isolate the affirmations that really mean something to you and say them daily as if they are already fact.

THOUGHT QUESTIONS TO PROBE YOUR MIND

1. Can you recall three negative affirmations you have fallen into the habit of repeating? Bring them to the front of your mind and think seriously about how they are hurting you.

2. Have you heard others affirm negatively about their own work lives.?

3. Do you ever think of your mind as a computer capable of being programmed? If you could choose programs for your brain, what kind would you select? How much responsibility are you willing to take for the information that goes into your mind? Are you willing to let others program you, or do you want to program yourself?

MYTH NUMBER SEVEN

*Women encounter too many
blocks and problems at
work to gain real momentum
in getting ahead.*

A WOMAN AT WORK

"I should have quit a dozen times, but, thank goodness, I didn't know it."

Linda Nelson can joke now about the first three years of her jewelry business, but in 1975, things weren't so funny. She started making jewelry seriously after her homemade earrings became the most popular item at her Women's Club Spring Festival. Her booth was out of stock in an hour, but Linda had the foresight to keep back a few samples and take orders the rest of the day. The next problem was filling the orders and figuring out how to get more. Friends and family encouraged her, but Linda insists no one really thought a housewife could get much further than a garage studio and a few orders from the community. Linda's tone makes it obvious that she had as much fun proving she was able to build a business as she had in actually doing it. Her husband got interested in the effort, and together they traveled to endless and exhausting craft and trade shows to set up Linda's booth and take orders. During these first years of traveling, their file of customers grew into a substantial mailing list. Linda's creative energy surged during this period, and her designs became more and more popular. Next, she put together a small mailing catalog to serve the customers she had met while selling in different cities, and that's how she broke into mail order. It was a short step to display ads in magazines and purchased mailing lists. The nicest breakthrough, though, was in capturing the interest of retail stores. Linda's biggest business problem these days is distributing her jewelry. Employees handle it very well, but Linda says she

91

retains worrying rights. Her most important current functions in the business are the two things she does best, designing and selling. What happened to her family along the way? They're all working in a $3,000,000.00 jewelry business started in a garage storage room by a simple (don't you believe it) housewife.

MYTH NUMBER SEVEN
Women encounter too many blocks and problems at work to gain real momentum in getting ahead.

REALITY

Solutions to work related problems are bound up in the application of two kinds of skills; people skills and technical skills. You must concentrate on developing both if you plan to advance. As you attempt to work through technical and people problems, keep the points below in mind. They will help you avoid becoming immobilized:

- It's never too early or too late in your career to seek creative solutions to problems.

- Don't be mentally and emotionally undone by blocks and problems. Everyone experiences them and everyone has to figure out how to cope. When you feel like you're drowning in problems, remember you are not alone.

- Dreaming up workable strategies to solve career problems is not a knack or an art form. It is a learnable skill that improves with practice.

- Any strategy you use must be implemented with sensitivity to timing, personalities involved, formal company rules and regulations, and informal company rules and regulations. Remember, your actions are not without context.

BENEFITS OF DISPELLING THE MYTH

Debunking the myth that problems at work prevent women from gaining momentum helps you realize that this is only true when women don't recognize the need for developing competence in problem solving. In trying to work out a personal style for dealing with blocks and problems, you need to consider the following:

• Problems are inevitable. You cannot escape them.

• Every job has a unique set of problems. Therefore, whether you're on your first job or whether you've changed jobs ten times, you can always expect problems to appear.

• Developing the ability to handle problems smoothly is a valuable skill in the working world. Anyone can manage regular tasks and schedules, but it takes a special person to keep people and work under control when things go wrong. With a little practice, you can be that kind of person.

• A crisis has the potential to make you look like a genius or an idiot, depending on how you choose to work through it. Did you notice the word, choose, in the previous sentence? It was used to emphasize the point that you really do have a choice of behaving sensibly or foolishly during a crisis. If you pretend otherwise, you are only deceiving yourself.

KEY POINTERS

Approach problems as opportunities instead of disasters and you'll put yourself in an entirely different category from most of your co-workers. Remember, it's not the problems, it's how you handle them that counts. Cool heads prevail, so let the coolest head be yours.

STRATEGIES FOR BROADENING YOUR CAREER HORIZON

Dealing with career blocks and problems calls for the use of many options. Consider the following examples of ways to unblock conditions which impede progress. The strategies suggested will stimulate you to think creatively about formulating your own strategic options.

BLOCK

• Can't get a job at all or can't get the job you want.

STRATEGIC OPTIONS

• New graduates often run into trouble in this area, but seasoned workers sometimes suffer from it, too. What can you do about it? First, stop whining and complaining. Recently, a college graduate stated angrily on a nationally televised talk show that she had been to 52 interviews over 18 months and still had no job. This is not the kind of language that motivates contacts to recommend you or employers to hire you. If you can't find a job, take it as your responsibility to analyze and correct your approach to employers. Don't think employers ought to tailor their requirements to meet your personal needs. It won't happen, so don't expect it.

BLOCK

• Don't know how to find out what's available.

STRATEGIC OPTIONS

• Responding to want ads and registering with employment agencies can be productive, but more and better jobs are found through personal contacts. Make a job contact list of friends, relatives, people you know from other jobs you've held, contacts in professional organizations, friends you've made in seminar and training sessions, and anyone else who might be in the position of hearing about a good job. Start asking your contacts for help. It's an accepted job hunting practice, but be sure you ask in a positive and professional manner. You can't honestly expect anyone to refer you if they aren't sure you will reflect well on them. Try to have your contacts perceive you in the best light possible.

• As you work your contacts, think about the young woman who went to 52 fruitless interviews. This means she now knows 52 people whose job responsibilities include hiring others. There is no doubt that an analysis of these interviews would reveal their value goes far beyond consideration for the job at hand. Ask yourself the following questions to determine the real worth of a specific interview:

1. In developing your list of contacts, did you include people who have interviewed you for jobs you didn't get?

2. Are you aware of the levels of evaluation going on in interviews? For example, interviewers will most likely be in the position of knowing about different jobs as they come open in their companies. If you project a profes-

sional attitude in your interview, you will be remembered and you may be considered for a job other than the one for which you applied.

- Do you think contacts are worth keeping warm even when you're not in the market for a job? Here is where networking is most abused. People too often use contacts, get what they're after, and then immediately drop the people who helped them. Those who are guilty of this never realize for themselves or others the full benefit of networking.

- Do you understand there is no disgrace in taking a job for which you're over qualified just to get your foot in the door, meet people, and establish yourself as a hard worker?

BLOCK

- Don't know how to apply or interview for jobs.

STRATEGIC OPTIONS

- You need to learn how to package yourself properly. Resumes, cover letters, thank you notes, and all other correspondence with potential employers must express a high level of professionalism. Concise and courteous written communications are appreciated. Use them, but also use personal visits and the telephone to further your job hunting cause. Think of your efforts as having two purposes; first getting appointments and then getting a job. An appointment doesn't necessarily have to be focused on a specific job. It may be exploratory in nature, at the same time giving you an excellent opportunity to put your best foot forward. People who hire keep files on good job candidates, and make no mistake about it, they will evaluate you closely even if they are not interviewing you for a specific job. Do your best to make a good impression. Use the following checklist as you prepare for interviews or for appointments with people who can help you with leads.

1. Good use of professional looking written communications.

2. Pleasant and professional telephone usage.

   • Give your name immediately when you make business calls. It's also helpful to relate why you're calling.

   • Answer the phone with a greeting and your name.

   • Be careful about asking people to return calls. They often can't or won't, and then you're in the position of waiting for a phone call that never comes. Try asking when it would be convenient for you to call back.

3. Good anticipation of questions.

   • Make a written list of the questions you might be asked.

   • Write your answers and work in points you want to make about your experience, training, and aspirations. Keep your answers short and to the point. Avoid rambling. If you don't know the answer to a question, say, "I don't know, but I will try to find out if you'd like."

   Example of a Typical Interview
   Question and a Good Response

   Q. You've been working as a receptionist for two years which gives you no experience in managing other people. What makes you think you could make the transition to office manager?

A. Yes, I have been a receptionist for two years, but my duties covered much more than answering the phone. I was responsible for the appointment book, billing clients, and paying office bills. We had a high rate of absenteeism and turnover the first year I had the job, and I often found myself filling in as secretary to one or more of the four lawyers in our office. We also had a lot of temporary help coming in as a result of the absenteeism, and it always fell to me to train them. During my second year, my boss and I worked out an arrangement so the secretaries could have some scheduled time off instead of having to call in sick all the time. We also hired a part-time person to do relief work so we wouldn't have so many temporaries in and out of the office. My boss was very satisfied with my work on these innovations, and I'm certain I could do just as well in handling the responsibilities of office manager.

4. Make out your own list of questions that apply to whatever appointment or interview for which you are preparing. You can take this list with you and jot down answers in the meeting. Any sort of written agenda or list of questions, plus note taking, gives you a more organized and serious look.

EXAMPLES OF GOOD QUESTIONS
TO ASK IN AN INTERVIEW

- To whom would I be reporting directly?

- Will there be any training opportunities to help me do a better job?

- What training would you recommend for me to complete on my own to better prepare myself for this job or other jobs in your firm?

BLOCK

Can't compete with other applicants because of lack of experience or training.

STRATEGIC OPTIONS

If you truly don't have adequate skills to land the job you want, go after a lower echelon job and immediately get yourself into some kind of skill building program designed to prepare you for the working world. Watch the newspaper for available classes, look in the yellow pages under education and instruction, and call colleges and technical schools to find out what they offer in the area of career planning and development. You have to look and ask for help before you can expect to get help.

BLOCK

Unable to present characteristics which counter balance other inadequacies.

STRATEGIC OPTIONS

- Perhaps you don't have very much work experience, but you were reared by parents who always worked hard, made their own way, and who encouraged you to do the same. Find a way to mention these values in an interview.

• Perhaps you have not actually worked in management, but you have taken night courses and seminars in this area over the past two years. In an interview, point to your student based competency and assert your intention to keep training. Your persistence will pay off.

• Always lead with strength. In areas where you are strong, be very strong. In areas where you are weak, be able to articulate how you intend to improve.

SUMMING UP

The blocks and strategic options outlined above relate generally to the ultimate problem of getting a job in the first place, and to the need for maintaining mobility in the work place once you break in. It was appropriate to make this limitation since virtually every other section of this guide offers creative strategies for dealing with problems that crop up after you are already on the job. Fortunately, we have all matured enough to wax philosophical when problems occur at work. We have realized that women experience special problems, but so do men, minorities, and other groups. Yes, women have had to do well on their jobs, and, at the same time, continually prove they are serious about career and advancement. This has been a very real and sometimes emotionally draining situation, but I maintain we would do well to simply acknowledge it as a part of the real world of work. If we approach it as just another problem to work through, we will have a better chance of overcoming it.

THOUGHT QUESTIONS TO PROBE YOUR MIND

1. How do you think the concept known as the transferral of ideas would relate to solving career problems?

2. How would you interpret the following quote? "It doesn't matter whether they occur at work or at home, problems are all the same."

3. Think of a specific work related problem you have right now and pretend it belongs to someone else. Name at least three ways to approach the problem and decide which one should be tried first.

4. If you make more money than your spouse, what are a few strategies that could be used to keep this from becoming a problem? Do you think there are people, male or female, who actually enjoy having a problem develop in this area? Why?

MYTH NUMBER EIGHT

Gaining visibility with people who make decisions is almost impossible for women at work.

A WOMAN AT WORK

"I didn't have anyone to teach me how to get raises and promotions, so I learned by imitating my boss and other company executives. Nobody told me to do that, but I'm glad I did because it worked very well."

Carol Woodruff assumed the role of chief breadwinner in her family when she had to take a job to put her husband through college. Her position as secretary in a large recreational vehicle company headquarters didn't pay too well, so she immediately started looking for ways to improve her salary. She learned quickly that the best way to stand out and gain visibility was to become a clever mimic. She patterned her own image by those of her superiors, which meant she had to concentrate on many details that were ignored by her equals. Offering new ideas, being on time with assignments, dressing like management, volunteering for push jobs, and executing them successfully. These were but a few angles Carol employed to make herself known. By the time her husband got his degree, Carol was being called on regularly by company execs to help with special assignments, in addition to serving as office manager for the secretarial pool. Her title, which she dreamed up herself and requested along with her last sizable raise, is Special Project Coordinator. That's not bad for a woman who started working just to help her husband. Do you think she quit her job when he graduated? *No way.*

MYTH NUMBER EIGHT
Gaining visibility with people who make decisions is almost impossible for women at work.

REALITY

Gaining visibility at work is becoming less and less elusive for women. Smart women are not only succeeding at being noticed and remembered, they are often doing it better than their male counterparts. Men are expected to try hard and excel in their jobs. Therefore, it doesn't seem unusual when they do. But women who excel are still in the fortunate position of creating a stir. A hard working male executive is just another hard working guy, but a hard working female executive is viewed as exceptional. And a hard working black female executive is considered practically superhuman. If you approach work as men do, you will be considered a real go getter. If you go just a little further and activate a carefully orchestrated, systematic process toward significant advancement in your career, you will be considered brilliant. It's like being the only girl on the baseball team. Who do you think gets written up in the newspaper? The value of positive visibility is great enough to attract much competition for its benefits. Companies don't pay $500,000.00 a minute for prime TV advertising time because visibility isn't important. It is very important, and if you haven't figured out how to capture it yet, now is the time to learn.

BENEFITS OF DISPELLING THE MYTH

Debunking the myth that gaining visibility is impossible for women opens the door to literally hundreds of opportunities. In taking advantage of these opportunities, you would be wise to keep in mind the following sensitivities:

- Visibility without credibility is worthless. If you aren't willing to deliver the goods in substantive work, don't shoot your mouth off around people who are in a position to evaluate and make decisions about employees.

- You are not the only one seeking visibility. Competition is stiff. Also, don't think people won't realize what you're after.

- Many times helping your boss, co-workers, and your company gain recognition can be the perfect avenue to being recognized yourself.

- Characteristics like sincerity, integrity, and a willingness to help others will enhance your efforts to be noticed. Phoniness, excessive selfishness, or an inflated ego may help you succeed in being remembered, but not in the way you'd like.

STRATEGIES TO BROADEN YOUR CAREER HORIZON

1. To become more visible, observe your superiors' schedules and look for chances to see them "accidentally." Sometimes arriving at work a few minutes early or staying a few minutes late will provide informal time for you to chat casually with superiors. This will also set you

apart as one who doesn't mind giving extra time and preparation to work.

2. Try arriving early for meetings. You may get a chance to get to know individuals in charge of the sessions.

3. Volunteer to serve on committees with groups that include management in the membership. For example, if your company has a committee organized to encourage communications between line and staff employees, volunteer to serve on the committee as a representative from your department.

4. Learn to use memos and reports to communicate with your boss and subordinates. Keep messages concise, to the point, dated, and extremely courteous in tone. Having all your colleagues know you keep a neat and orderly file of documented communications is a very polite and effective way of keeping everyone honest about whose ideas are whose.

5. Send written communications to superiors when appropriate; congratulations, interesting articles or clippings, thank you notes, positive comments on their recent speeches, meetings, and new plans for the company. Be sincere, specific, and brief.

6. Take a class or seminar related to your department's key concerns. Let your boss know what you're studying and ask if she would like you to conduct a mini-workshop on the new information you've learned in your course.

7. Watch for areas of responsibility you might take over for your boss, or better yet, initiate a new program designed to increase sales or efficiency.

8. Understand that being used and abused is one thing, but being willing to do menial tasks to get the job done is another. Grasping the difference in these two things takes real sensitivity and can make or break you in your work setting. Here is where observing the habits and attitudes of someone you respect can help you. I've seen company presidents shove chairs and tables around to make a room more comfortable for a meeting. If they can do menial tasks, so can you.

9. Be an attentive listener and ask good questions. Whether talking with an individual or participating in a group meeting, well thought out questions can upgrade your chances of being remembered. Beware of pointless, argumentative, or ax grinding comments and questions designed simply to draw attention to yourself, and don't try to steal the show or keep the floor. Do exercise good judgment in timing, phrasing, and articulating thoughtful questions so you come off looking helpful and interested instead of egotistical or adversative.

10. Always project a professional image at work. Your appearance, attitudes, communication skills, and work habits speak volumes. You must attend to these meticulously. However, they can only be of partial benefit if you aren't willing to show them off. You don't have to be a glory hog to acquire the kind of attention getting ahead requires, but you can't be a wallflower, either. Think creatively about how to become a known entity, especially to people who make decisions. They don't automatically know or remember how great you are, so you have to remind them regularly and tastefully.

11. Every time you express an idea or suggest a change, remember to include an implementation plan. It sets you apart from idea junkies who talk great ideas but can't put them into positive action.

KEY POINTERS

Properly packaged women who try to achieve career visibility by using planned, systematic processes can expect to see excellent results. What does properly packaged mean? In simple terms, it means tailoring your appearance, skills, contacts, paper (credentials, functional resumes, business cards, brochures, portfolios of projects, recommendations, photos, etc.), speech, writing, and experience to the career area in which you want to advance.

THOUGHT QUESTIONS TO PROBE YOUR MIND

1. Your friend complains to you that she and a co-worker were in line for the same promotion, but the co-worker got it "just because she throws herself in the boss's path every chance she gets." What would you say to your friend about going after her own visibility? Name three specific tactics you would advise her to employ.

2. Aside from the information in the course itself, what would be the value of taking a course or seminar for people in levels of work above yours?

3. How might you attend a meeting and show off your preparedness without having to speak excessively?

MYTH NUMBER NINE

There is a clear-cut path to advancement and success.

A WOMAN AT WORK

"My only problem has been coordinating my skills with my ambition. There really wasn't a track for me to follow, so I had to forge my own path."

Marjorie Sanders is proud of the twists and turns in her career development. They attest to her steadfast confidence in her own good judgment. Marjorie started out in the military where she received extensive training as a public information specialist. Her experience in this area helped her land a civilian job with a public relations firm when she finished her last tour of duty. However, Marjorie wanted to do something more daring than simply changing employers. That's why she spent so much time away from her job trying to get other firms to hire her as a public relations consultant. She was fired for this forthwith, and efforts toward marketing herself as a consultant had to be stepped up considerably. At the same time, she started her executive services business which offers typing, business addresses and mail boxes, plus an answering service. Marjorie's efforts have paid off steadily in securing consulting clients and in marketing her executive services business, and she insists that finding the courage to conquer her fear of changing work venues and environments has been the key to her success.

MYTH NUMBER NINE
There is a clear-cut path to advancement and success.

REALITY

Advancing at work results from managing many different processes all of which must be adapted to individual situations and styles. These processes don't always yield quick and easy gratification, but don't let that fool you. Keep at it and the rewards will come. You cannot do A, B, C, and instantly experience X, Y, Z. Your efforts must have time to develop, so don't abandon them. Scurrying about from activity to activity and then complaining that nothing works insures many of your efforts will end in frustration. You can avoid this by sticking with productive behaviors once you've started them. If they've worked for others, they can work for you. Be patient and tenacious enough to see them to fruition.

BENEFITS OF DISPELLING THE MYTH

Debunking the myth that there is a clear-cut path to advancement allays gnawing fears. These fears can lead to an inability to make the decisions necessary to move forward, but you can overcome this by taking action. Since anxiety, uncertainty, and fear are relieved when you do something about them, use three simple tactics to calm your mind; (a) confront fears, (b) put them in perspective, and (c) realize you are not alone in experiencing anxiety and fears.

The following analyses of a few common fears will help you deal with your own troublesome apprehensions:

- You no longer have to be afraid you are the only one who doesn't know exactly what to do to get ahead. Women have suffered from this fear for decades because their traditional responsibilities at work seldom required skills in decision making. We have always done what we were told, assuming all the while that the people doing the telling knew what they were talking about. Admittedly, it's a bit disconcerting to find out bosses don't always know if they are right or wrong, but understanding this fact can help you get over your own fear of making decisions. It also frees you from thinking there are absolute right and wrong decisions, and introduces you to thinking in terms of a long continuum of reasonable choices. In actuality, sound decisions are usually somewhere between totally right and totally wrong, and you have more than enough brain power to think through all the gray areas and arrive at your own perfectly acceptable decisions.

- You no longer have to be unduly scared of failure. Again, our inexperience in the working world has led us to believe we are always supposed to get things right. Why should women set up such unrealistic expectations? The important thing is to give ourselves plenty of chances to learn from mistakes and to try again.

- You should not worry that you can't handle career and family responsibilities at the same time. Your family life is not going to be perfect if you stay at home all the time, and it's not going to be perfect if you work. What it can be is reasonable, workable, manageable, and even enjoyable, but never, never perfect. The only solution to this dilemma is to set priorities, do what you can to accomplish them, be flexible, and *let the rest go.*

KEY POINTERS

- Certain basics exist which you must comprehend.

   1. Searching for the easy path to success is futile. It's much better to expect success via a series of planned and then continually modified activities.

   2. Important career and business decisions are never without some risk and chance for failure. If a planned action doesn't get the result you want, change your course and keep going.

- As you grow in the world of work, you will benefit from resisting the tendency to try to put everything and everyone into rigid formulas and categories.

- The ability to live with ambiguity, cope with ambiguity, and deal effectively with ambiguity is a mark of real maturity.

123

STRATEGIES FOR BROADENING
YOUR CAREER HORIZON

• Search out or organize a small group of women like yourself who listen, talk, encourage, suggest, support, nurture, and love, but who never evaluate or judge. Of course, building a base of male and female business contacts (networking) is vital, but it fills a different need than an intimate group who really try to help each other integrate their insides with their images.

• Seek mentors above your level who are willing to offer guidance and counseling based on their experience.

• As much as you possibly can, stay away from critics, doom and gloom predictors, and nay sayers. Avoiding this kind of person is a healthy strategy for you, so don't feel guilty about it.

• Do the hardest things first to keep from wasting time and energy fearing or worrying about them.

• Don't over analyze. If you face a delicate situation, such as speaking before a group, approach it mechanically. Preparing and organizing beats worrying in two ways: (1) It takes away the anxiety of feeling unprepared, and (2) it keeps you too busy to worry.

• Other than planning for basic contingencies, focus your energy on going forward instead of fretting over what might happen. Simply, contingency planning means lining up reasonable backup options. For example, it makes sense to prepare for questions from your audience when you speak publicly, but it isn't feasible to try and think of every possible question. Again, go forward or you will end up suffering paralysis from analysis.

THOUGHT QUESTIONS TO PROBE YOUR MIND

1. Where would you go for help if you encountered what seemed to be an insurmountable problem at work?

2. If you found yourself assigned to a project in some unclear capacity, what are some alternatives for dealing with not knowing exactly what's expected of you?

3. What is your working definition of contingency planning?

MYTH NUMBER TEN

Big corporations offer the best opportunities.

TWO WOMEN AT WORK

"Sometimes I have to laugh at the differences in Laura and me. I work so hard to maintain my corporate image, and she goes to work at her daycare center in sweat pants and a knit shirt. I'm sure she nets more money than I do, but that's all right because I could never have handled the risks she has taken. I really do admire Laura's spunk."

Ruth Metcalf doesn't realize her friend, Laura Mitchell, expresses the same sentiments about her. Laura feels Ruth displayed the superior courage by competing successfully in a big corporation. The truth is both women have much to be proud of even though their careers are going in very different directions.

Ruth graduated from college with a business degree and took a job with a large computer firm. She felt very secure within the structured environment and literally plodded her way to executive status by way of a pre-set track.

Laura dropped out of college after her first year because she couldn't get in step with all the rules and guidelines that go along with academic endeavors. She went to work at a day-care center as the lowest paid attendant and didn't go much further for over two years. What she did do, though, was learn every detail of the business from her boss who became her mentor. Over a period of years, most of the responsibilities of managing the business were turned over to Laura, and she also helped her boss expand the operation to two additional sites. When the boss wanted to retire, who

129

went to the bank and secured financing to buy her out? None other than our college dropout, Laura Mitchell.

MYTH NUMBER TEN
Big corporations offer the best opportunities.

REALITY

Some do... some don't. But let's not forget the real business of corporations is business, not mapping out career paths for employees. The profit motive has had a wonderful side effect of serving the nation's economy and providing jobs. However, this fit would never have occurred, and certainly won't last, if the basic needs of the corporation are choked off by demands of employees. It is a symbiotic relationship that must be understood by individuals who aspire to get ahead in the corporate structure. Smart women have carefully analyzed their places in the big picture of corporate life. Their astute examination and analysis have helped them decide if they are going in the right direction. You have to do the same analyzing and deciding for yourself. No one is going to do it for you. Others can advise, encourage, and help you, but ultimately, you must make and live with your own decisions based on your own well thought out conclusions. Things are improving for women who elect to join large corporations, but there are some realities that can't be ignored. For instance, the woman who goes back to school in her late thirties and earns a business degree by age forty will be competing with twenty-two year old graduates for entry level jobs in big business. She can't really expect to start at the same level as men and women who have already been working twenty years just because she is the same age. This reality, plus a range of others, contributes to career problems for women whose skills, experience, age, and ambition are incompatible with the needs of large corporations. If you fall in this category, for whatever reason, your career energy might best be spent in a framework other than a large company.

BENEFITS OF DISPELLING THE MYTH

Debunking the myth that big corporations offer the best opportunities paves the way to success for women who are not bound for the boardroom. It also reinforces the idea that tried and true strategies for getting ahead are useful across career lines. In other words, precepts and principles for advancement remain the same wherever you are working.

Another benefit of debunking the myth that big corporations offer the only route to success is a new awareness of basic differences in working for large or small businesses. Understanding these differences is a necessary prerequisite to deciding which setting is right for you. Consider the following advantages and disadvantages of working in three kinds of organizational structures; large corporations or agencies, small businesses, and entrepreneurial enterprises. Perhaps you will gain insight as to which structure complements your particular strengths and weaknesses.

I. LARGE CORPORATIONS AND AGENCIES

ADVANTAGES	DISADVANTAGES
Job security	Large numbers of people competing for a relatively small number of advancement opportunities.
Necessary steps to advancement are easy to plot because they are generally known.	Criteria regarding age, years in the field, experience, and training are strictly adhered to in making advancement decisions.

133

Benefits such as health insurance, retirement programs, sick leave, and vacations are part of the job package.

Jobs are highly categorized and usually offer a set range of responsibilities at each level. Also, salaries, benefits, and schedules are not readily negotiable.

II. SMALL BUSINESSES

ADVANTAGES

DISADVANTAGES

Since there is a small number of jobs, each one covers several areas of responsibility. This provides for a wide range of experience over a short period of time.

Small businesses are not as stable as large corporations or agencies. Therefore, job security is lessened.

Salaries, schedules, and responsibilities are more negotiable because decision makers are not bound by rigid rules and policies.

Job settings can be too close for comfort, causing personalities to clash and work problems to intensify.

Requirements for employment are more flexible. Therefore, people who don't fit absolute standards can still expect reasonable consideration for jobs.

Incompetent employees are hard to phase out when the company you work for is supposed to be a small, happy family.

III. ENTREPRENEURIAL ENTERPRISES

ADVANTAGES	DISADVANTAGES
Set your own hours. Be your own boss. Enjoy fewer age, sex, experience, and training limitations.	Requires an enormous amount of energy and discipline to make the work effort consistent and productive.
Opportunity to earn more money.	Overhead is increased and benefits (health insurance, retirement, etc.) have to be paid out of pocket.
Opportunity to build a business of your own and provide employment for others.	Great risks are involved. Entrepreneurial activities are not for the faint hearted.

KEY POINTERS

We live in an age when doors are opening wide for women who want to move up the corporate ladder, but some of us don't fit into corporate life no matter what creative strategies we devise. If you find yourself in this position, don't despair. Other avenues exist for you, avenues that have just as much and maybe more potential as moving through the ranks of a big bureaucracy.

STRATEGIES FOR BROADENING YOUR CAREER HORIZON

• Take stock of your values, training, career aspirations, and commitment in terms of varied work settings. Be brutally honest about what you want, what you have to offer, and what you think you can return. On the other hand, don't discount things you haven't tried before. Stretching your abilities provides more growth than clinging to a worn out skill base, so include in your self assessment an intangible known as the willingness to grow and learn. Keep in mind that if you can't articulate to yourself or on paper what it is you have to offer, you're not going to be able to convince others of your value. Self assess. It will crystallize in your mind exactly what you are all about, and that is the first step in persuading others to have confidence in you.

• Ask people who know you well where they think you'd do best. Describe the three broad areas you're researching; large corporations, small businesses, and entrepreneurial enterprises, and solicit opinions on which area seems to be the natural place for you. Someone may come up with a good suggestion. Keep your mind open to the creative thoughts of other people as they will often encourage you to do things they'd like to do themselves. Many times people won't follow their own advice because they don't have the courage, not because they think their suggestions are unsound. Courage comes from confidence, and confidence comes from preparedness. Do your homework in the area of self evaluation, and you'll have an edge on the preparation necessary to make courageous decisions about your career.

• Do research. Interview people who work in differing environments. Think about which of these people you relate to best. Check your assumptions and theories against their first hand experiences. Look for discrepancies and consider how you would handle them if you had to.

• Determine which career related articles and books interest you most. You may have a pattern that you haven't identified yet. Monitor your reading habits to decide which areas spark your imagination.

- Attend meetings and conferences that draw participants from alternative organizations. Identify which of the attendees you get along with best and which of their work settings intrigue you most.

- Write or call a few key executives from different sized businesses and ask them how they evaluate prospective employees. Consider your own congruence with what you find out.

- In the process of collecting information, be totally frank with yourself about the advantages and disadvantages of each work setting you examine. Your candor will support the correctness of personal career decisions.

- Illusions and realities exist in every job. Thus, you need to be aware of falling victim to selective curiosity. You need to know the good and the bad, so make it a definite part of your search to identify the illusions which may initially capture your imagination. It's a long way down when a dazzling job confronts you with some miserable realities. If you can fine tune your expectations to fit what is real, you'll be happier with your decisions and choices. This is not to say you should expect little or nothing from your career. Women have already done that too long. It's a matter of aligning what you want with what you can actually get, and then maximizing your chances for achieving it.

- Remember, no career is totally devoid of tedium, difficulties, and problems. Whether just beginning or whether contemplating a change, you can count on putting up with a certain level of pure aggravation. Knowing

137

this to start with may help you avoid being blindsided with problems you didn't expect. You'll be able to deal with them more effectively.

• When you finally select a work environment suited to your stage of development, prepare a portfolio which summarizes what you've learned in your explorations. You'll be better prepared to tell people who make decisions regarding jobs why you want to work in the environment you've chosen. From the comparative data you've gathered about work places, include a problem or two in your portfolio which you believe you could help solve. Don't go overboard, but using qualified language express how you would at least assist with a solution. Cap your discussion with well conceived questions and your stock will go up with interviewers and decision makers.

THOUGHT QUESTIONS TO PROBE YOUR MIND

1. What is your fit in the big picture of your work environment? Can you identify another environment where you'd rather work?

2. As you assess your values, interests, and skills, what type of organizational structure do you think is best for you?

3. Why do you think you can grow and advance to your fullest in the setting you selected in question two?

MYTH NUMBER ELEVEN

*Changing jobs or career fields
is extremely difficult,
fraught with pain, and
viewed as unprofessional.*

A WOMAN AT WORK

"What child wants a stale old burnout for a school teacher? I knew that's what I had become, but it took me quite a while to figure out what to do about it. Then one Sunday I spent the whole day clipping want ads from three different newspapers. That was the beginning of a year long job search, but it was worth the effort. Yes, ten years and two promotions later, I can definitely say it was worth it."

Dianne Harris has benefited from all the excitement and growth that comes with changing jobs, and she has done it without abandoning her chosen field of education. She hired a professional resume writer to help her prepare cover letters and resumes for each individual job she applied for. That way she could feature the skills most applicable to the job in question. Dianne is convinced this tactic, plus improving her performance in interviews, landed her a position as ancillary staff trainer in the inservice education program of a major hospital. At first her pay was lower than her teaching salary, but that was remedied in less than a year when she took over the position of assistant director. Her next major promotion occurred in four years when Dianne was asked to serve as director for the hospital's education program. A healthy raise, travel opportunities, and several other perks came with her new title and job, which explains very well why she is glad she had the courage ten years ago to make a sensible change.

MYTH NUMBER ELEVEN
Changing jobs or career fields is extremely difficult, fraught with pain, and viewed as unprofessional.

REALITY

There are times when change is the best alternative. It may be needed to stimulate new growth or to relieve deep seated discontent and frustration. Dealing with problems at work is something we all have to do, but real suffering isn't necessary. The key is to find a balance between the positives and the negatives. Women, in particular, put up with all manner of situations they should either change or leave. Fortunately, our career self concepts have now improved enough to allow us to seek better conditions.

If you're working in a setting that is making you miserable most of the time, start the processes necessary to make a change. Be sure however, that it really is your work that is the problem. Many people blame everything and everybody for problems they create for themselves. Make sure you're honest about what is really at the base of your dissatisfaction. If you want to advance, you can't dissipate energy on severe problems you are powerless to solve. It's better to face facts and move on than to spin your wheels trying to fix the unfixable. A healthy way to think about career or job change is to focus on the potential for excitement, fresh experiences, a different environment, meeting new people, and the opportunity for growth. After all, you don't want to change directions simply to get rid of things you don't like. It would be better to make changes based on forward, positive thinking. There's nothing wrong with trying to escape a bad situation, but make significant career changes based on what you're going toward, not what you're leaving behind.

BENEFITS OF DISPELLING THE MYTH

Debunking the myth that changing jobs or careers is too difficult routs the fears surrounding it. Competent women are finding the courage to analyze their career situations and make sensible changes. They no longer accept being stereotyped, nor do they allow themselves to be locked into inflexible career tracks. Smart, competent women understand the concepts of process, interrelationships, and the give and take of problem solving. They have become experts at the application of this knowledge, and they know when and how to use it in advancing themselves in their current work. More importantly, they know how to use it in making successful career or job changes. Fear is no longer their jailer, and limitations are no longer their focus. They have learned how to (a) anticipate events and peoples' reactions, (b) recognize what is and isn't working, (c) make decisions to change directions and cut losses, and (d) implement change in ways that are profitable to themselves.

STRATEGIES FOR BROADENING YOUR CAREER HORIZON

Some legitimate reasons for seeking job changes are listed below. You're going to run into some of them in every job, but struggling with too many at a time will definitely inhibit your progress. As you read through the list, evaluate your own environment as to conduciveness to growth and advancement. If you find your situation skewed toward hopeless or serious problems, plan to make a change. Do it professionally and tactfully, but do it.

REASONS AND SITUATIONS WHICH INDICATE A CHANGE IS NEEDED

- Poor staffing. (There's nothing wrong with working for a while in an area that doesn't match your skills and strengths, but if you find yourself doing it too long, you need to take action.)

- Poorly organized environment. (You can use this to your advantage if your contributions toward better organization are noticed by decision makers. Keep written records of your improvements and projects. Then, if you can't get recognition for what you've learned and implemented in your present job, use your knowledge to create a better resume and improve your interviews when you go after the next job.)

- Poor supervision. (This one can be a killer if you aren't accustomed to figuring out a course and then following it on your own. Not knowing what you're supposed to do can create great anxiety. However, if you manage to do a few things right by yourself, you may end up looking better than if you had been required to follow a set formula. Whether or not poor supervision is a serious problem also depends on whether it equates to little supervision, confusing supervision, or harsh supervision. Only you can make the final analysis about your particular situation, and only you can decide if it's intolerable. Trust your own judgment.)

- Unclear reward systems and obscure routes to advancement. (This situation might be a problem to some people and an advantage to others. Carving out your own territory can be stimulating if you are able to persuade your superiors to support and reward you for your ideas and for your success in executing them. You may even have to dream up and request your own rewards. The rub comes when superiors aren't open to having subordinates initiate change or make requests. I've always gone forward on the assumption that intelligent people are open to new ideas well presented. However, very often the inability to get people to consider new ideas is connected either to the quality of the ideas themselves or the way in which they are presented. Evaluate your ability in this area before you complain too loudly about unclear reward systems and obscure routes to advancement. Maybe you can think of better ways to work around the ambiguity. If you're sure you cannot, don't waste your time complaining. Get busy and find a place to work where you can.)

• Individuals and cliques who create conflict and who purposely upset interpersonal relationships. (There are two areas of study which offer help in easing people problems. One is conflict management and the other is group dynamics. Let's take a look at managing conflict first. The ability to defuse anger, hostility, and sensitive situations is a golden skill. To acquire it, however, you must first learn to control yourself. Emotions are much affected by rest, diet, and exercise, so don't shortchange yourself in these very important areas. Another way to avoid sensitive situations is to guard against being baited by others. Allowing yourself to be lured into arguments is a classic example of being controlled by others. When you sense trouble brewing, concentrate very hard on speaking slowly, quietly, and in an even tone. Breathe in and out slowly and avoid gesticulating. It's also important that you learn some key counseling phrases to counter verbal attacks in a positive way. Practice starting your responses with the following phrases:

"A lot of people have probably felt as you do, but perhaps. . ."

"Have you ever considered. . ."

"I can see you feel badly about this. Why don't we. . ."

"I could certainly use your help in working through this problem because I'm at a loss as to how to make it right. What do you think. . ."

Now let's consider how the study of group dynamics can help. Group dynamics teaches us that many times work settings spawn rivalries between individuals or groups who try to instigate conflict surreptitiously. Motives stem from jealousy, competition, basic incompetence, lack of integrity, problems with the opposite sex, and difficulties with the work itself. You may even occasionally fall victim to one or two of these frailties yourself, but do your best to keep it to a minimum. Try to stay clear of problems and the people who cause them by focusing on your work and avoiding excessive groupiness. Make it a point to be genuinely friendly toward everyone in your work place, but make sure you maintain a serious and professional identity of your own. Never forget how you want to be viewed, and always behave accordingly. However, if individuals and cliques are continually destroying your efforts, move on. You will certainly encounter interpersonal problems wherever you work, but it's your responsibility to find a setting where they aren't intense enough to hold you back. You also need to continually improve your deftness at handling interpersonals.)

- Inadequate or unfair evaluation systems. (Evaluation systems fall into two categories, formal and informal. The real purpose behind them is to foster improvement, but many times they backfire and cause nothing but ill will. Improving the situation may not be possible, but it's worth a try before making the decision to leave because of it. Does your employer use a checklist and a one on one meeting to let you know which areas of your work are satisfactory and which areas need improvement? If so, ask if you might attach an addendum, agreed to by the two of you, of course, to the evaluation document. Then produce a few short paragraphs describing positive things you've accomplished that are not covered by the checklist. In an evaluation conference, always ask where you need to improve and later make a few specific written comments about what you intend to do during the next evaluation period to enhance your value to the company. Give a copy to your boss for placement in your personnel file. This will give you something to point to in your next meeting if you discipline yourself to follow through on what you wrote. Sooner or later you'll have to decide whether the evaluation process where you work is helping or hindering you. If you honestly feel the evaluation process is holding you back, marshall your forces and make a change.)

- Limited or no teamwork. (Careers don't get built in a vacuum. Therefore, teamwork must be employed. You can and should foster it no matter what your level of responsibility, but the cold fact is you are still subject to the philosophies of management. Employees have to be encouraged and taught to function as a team, and if your company hasn't caught onto this yet, it may not be the company to stay with for the long haul.)

• Poorly trained superiors and subordinates. (Money is usually at the root of this problem. Poorly trained employees come cheaper than skilled people. The trouble is that their lack of productivity matches their low price tags. Companies which habitually hire poorly trained people, and then make little effort to help them improve, often manifest other debilitating characteristics. Low creativity, unclear goals, lack of motivation, little effort to improve, no planning, negative disposition toward change, and poor hiring systems are but an unfortunate few. You should extricate yourself immediately from this kind of environment. Don't equivocate; just get out.)

THOUGHT QUESTIONS TO PROBE YOUR MIND

1. What is the basic difference between a hotheaded approach and a process approach to change?

2. How would you explain the phrase, "burning bridges behind you?" How does it relate to job or career changes?

3. Think about the women you know who have made significant and successful work changes. Were many of their skills transferrable? Which of your skills would fit into other career areas?

4. Are you intrigued by the notion of a career change? Try to articulate why you answered the way you did.

MYTH NUMBER TWELVE

*A fine education is the
ticket to success.*

A WOMAN AT WORK

"The friends I made in medical school were all like me, very goal oriented. My problem was that I got caught up in the goals of the group instead of really analyzing my own needs. Graduating was the only thing I focused on, forgetting entirely that there is, indeed, life after med school. It wasn't until after I finished that it struck me to change directions. It was painful, but I finally faced the fact that a career in medicine was not going to make me happy."

Cynthia Hollins never had any trouble actualizing goals. Her problem lay in distinguishing between goals she thought she ought to have and goals which were really in her own best interest. It took a lot of courage to walk into a career counseling office at a major university and admit to being a recent honor graduate from medical school who didn't want to be a doctor. These days Cynthia is working happily as a journalist. It took a lot of experimenting for her to settle into this field, but who knows? Maybe she'll make another career change next year.

MYTH NUMBER TWELVE
A *fine education is the ticket to success.*

REALITY

First of all, a good education does not necessarily begin and end within the confines of schools and colleges. Classroom training can be an excellent beginning, but the depth and quality of a really fine education can only result from a life long process of learning and application.

One of the most progressive, and now time honored, innovations on the career scene is the use of internships and cooperative education programs. Learning through the merger of classroom work and hands on experience has proven to be of exceptional value. The apprenticeship is also an old but useful educational device. Since experts agree that learning by doing is as important today as it ever was, perhaps you would do well to evaluate your own training opportunities in that context. The trick is to make sure your education does not take place in a vacuum. Therefore, choose your training experiences carefully because they are only useful if you can apply them in the real world. I will concede that many skills don't have to be restricted to one career area to be useful, but I stand on the premise that if you can't or won't apply the skills you learn, they will not do you much good.

BENEFITS OF DISPELLING THE MYTH

Debunking the myth that a fine education is the ticket to success will offer you a new perspective on selection of training and choice of career. With appropriate alternative training and work experience in your background, a full blown college education is not an absolute prerequisite to being successful. There is no question about it being a door opener (many employers won't consider hiring anyone without a college degree), but once you're hired, you have to prove your worth despite the quality of your credentials. But what should the job prove to you? Assuming you've sought training in a field which interests you in the first place, you still have no guarantee that your interests and values won't change. I would recommend that you always retain the psychological luxury of entertaining thoughts about varied career directions. It's healthy. Education is wonderful and I recommend it wholeheartedly, but sampling real work experience is far more enlightening. This is where you effectively test the following subtle and not so subtle dimensions of what you really want in a career:

- the integrity of what you assumed were your real interests and values.

- the sharpness of your skills.

- your vigor, energy, and ambition.

- the importance of specific personal needs such as money, security, prestige, leadership position, and work style.

- your innermost feelings about other career areas which may offer you more personal satisfaction.

STRATEGIES FOR BROADENING YOUR CAREER HORIZON

- Start by understanding the fact that there is no substitute for work experience as you develop marketable skills.

- Look at life broadly as a series of experiences all of which, when dissected, can teach you something applicable to your career.

- Do something, anything, to gain experience.

- Do it again.

- Carefully observe people who are doing well in various jobs. Interview them. Mimic them. Ask someone in a supposedly preferred career if you can tag along with him/her for half a day. Treat your own work and career research as a proving ground. Think seriously and realistically about which areas of work suit you best. Be candid about how successful you really think you could be in the various jobs you evaluate.

- Recognize that when you elect to try out different jobs, you will have to take risks and make mistakes, but you'll also do plenty right. Imagine yourself as being on a shake-down mission. You'll get the bugs out of your career system and be much the wiser for it. Go to libraries and study what professional associations are saying to their members in newsletters and periodicals. Find out what workers in the respective professions are concerned with or fighting about. Get a reading of frustrations workers confront in varying fields. Figure out the positives, too, but do it against the benchmark of reality. This kind of study is the next best thing to actually working in a particular field.

KEY POINTERS

- You must properly integrate experience with education if education itself is going to have real meaning to your career.

- Don't make an absolute career decision before you get a fair amount of work experience. Make only tentative decisions and go forward on a contingency basis.

- Break down the basic question of formal education versus experience by asking these two fundamental questions:

  1. After counseling, testing, and soul searching, what have I determined my skills, interests, and values to be?

  2. What will serve my skills, interests, and values best in terms of training and real work? (Perhaps some blend of the two would be a good choice.)

You probably find yourself unable to come up with absolute answers to the questions above. As you work through them, consider the wisdom that more complete answers may not emerge until you actually involve yourself in a bona fide educational program, and, at the same time or later on, some real work experience. A smart woman knows that experience is a great teacher. She is always connecting the learning from experience to her career goals. For example: If experience suggests that a particular job will never yield promotions or financial advancement, she will have no problem looking elsewhere. If experience suggests that only additional training will foster a successful job change or promotion, she will actively pursue the necessary training to upgrade herself.

• No linkage between experience and career goals can take place without action. Decisiveness is called for after you make the experience-goal connection, so make some ambitious decisions for yourself and follow up to make them work.

THOUGHT QUESTIONS TO PROBE YOUR MIND

1. Review the two questions in the preceding section. You must come to grips honestly with your true skills, interests, values, and priorities. Can you find any discrepancies in what you think they ought to be and what they really are?

2. Select a hypothetical career area you think may be right for you. Now try to identify several educational and work oriented experiences which would help you achieve success in this field. Where would you begin looking for the educational experience you've identified? Where would you seek the appropriate work experience?

3. Financially, what do you think would hurt more, a lack of education or a lack of experience?

4. Is promotion contingent upon education, experience, or both? Back up your answer with reasons.

5. Name several careers that require endless continuing education? Do you think all desirable careers have that characteristic?

SUCCESS FOR
WORKING WOMEN
and
TWELVE SECRETS
TO INSURE IT

SUCCESS FOR WORKING WOMEN

I am convinced there has never been a better time than now to be a working woman. It gives me pause to consider the great strides made by career women in recent decades, and I acknowledge with pride and gratitude that our new and unfolding opportunities stem directly from the hard work and commitment of courageous women who have gone before us. It is also gratifying to live in a time when men and women have learned to honor the full and varied potential of both sexes instead of relegating each other to stereotyped roles. Thus, we are all on the threshold, men and women alike, of enjoying a new spirit of cooperation and contribution.

Statistics prove women as a group are moving forward slowly but steadily in their careers. I believe this is largely the result of a new and voracious hunger to learn and use strategies that work for the future as well as for the present. This willingness to learn, change, grow, and develop makes a strong statement about our permanence in the world of work. We intend to persevere, to keep improving, and to pass on these closely held values to our children. We point with pride to new trends. U.S. corporations are actively recruiting up-and-coming female executives to their boards of directors. Heidrick and Struggles, a major executive search firm, recently reported in a study called, "The Changing Board," that in 1984, 49.6 percent of the Fortune 1,000 firms that were surveyed had at least one female director. This shows a great improvement from 43 percent in 1983, and 41.3 percent in 1982.

Interestingly, a current Wall Street Journal Gallup Survey notes that women who have made it to senior executive levels in their companies do not report racing to the top. On the contrary, these women say emphatically that their career climbs were slow and methodical. One fifty year old bank vice president relates that she started as a teller, then progressed to head teller, customer service rep., manager, and vice president. She maintains her personal ambition at work emerged late, and that many of her successes came through trial and error. Most of the other senior female executives described the same kind of unplanned development in their careers. Sixty-three percent of them were already working when they became interested in significant advancement, and many present female execs worked their way up from secretarial positions. I can only wonder what these outstanding women would have accomplished had they set out from the beginning to do something special with their careers.

Younger working women are planning earlier and better than their older colleagues. However, they have learned that no amount of planning, education, or strategizing can take the place of time and experience on the job, hard work, and dedication. They have also learned that competition is stiffening because it is becoming not only acceptable, but expected for women to pay as much attention to career development as men do. This is a healthy sign although somewhat scary in that it calls for regular updating of attitudes and behaviors. How fortunate that women already know how to be adaptable. As we make our marks in the world of work, we will use this trait to our benefit. How convenient that we have had so much practice in task oriented activities, detail work, making do, and picking up the slack. We will use this experience to lay unshakable foundations for our careers. As we go forward, let's be encouraged to use these attributes in every possible, conceivable way. We also need to continue our long tradition of gathering together all the positives and making the very best out of whatever situation is at hand. Finally, let's all be thankful that the new reality of career life for women has developed into such a wide range of achievable and desirable opportunities.

I have tried very hard to help you make your range of opportunities even broader. I have also tried to communicate on a personal level and to make room for a two way conversation between you and me on the pages of this book. Those of us who want to do well in our careers have so many things to talk over as we refine our efforts toward advancement. We have much to gain and much to offer by opening lines of communication and exchanging information. I'm extremely interested in your personal concerns about progress in your career. Please write to me and let me know how things are going for you. Again, I am interested.

Now I'd like to give you twelve secrets that have worked for me and for other women who are trying to make career progress. Use them and share them to help yourself and others achieve fulfillment and prosperity. Here's wishing you the best of luck in your quest.

TWELVE SECRETS

1. Successful career women make a habit of doing work related things unsuccessful women do not like to do.

   • You must get your hands dirty to get ahead. Don't avoid the distasteful tasks. Your boss probably didn't.

2. Being successful requires believing in yourself and in your company or organization.

   • You must feel you are choosing the right job for yourself and for those you serve to achieve true success.

3. An intelligent career woman will not divorce herself from sales and marketing roles.

   • Every aspect of sales and marketing should be understood, implemented, and/or accepted by an upward bound career woman. Sales and marketing make the economy work. You can't avoid it.

4. Your work habits will, in the final analysis, be the ingredient which will make or break your career.

   • People in management have known the positive or negative value of habits for years. Your habits are noticed. Make yours perfect.

5. Listening, writing, and speaking are skill areas in which you must excel.

   • The real world judges you mercilessly in these three areas. Your communication skills are critical to getting ahead. Don't assume you're skillful here. Get professional training in communications.

6. Become famous for your excellent questions.

   • People in the world of work respect astute, non-ax-grinding questions. Good questions help you make correct decisions.

7. Getting ahead career wise will mean change. Make any major change as simple as possible for yourself.

   • Studies of change in human behavior show that change is more easily accommodated the simpler it is. As you encounter career change, promotion, added responsibilities, and more complex assignments, don't overload your circuits by endless analysis or forecasting. Keep things simple and proceed step by step.

8. As you advance into management, leave your old job behind.

   • A critical mistake women make, as they go up the career ladder into management, involves the failure to understand that management means supervision. Too many women new in management cling to the old role and don't accept the new one. Doing your old job in your new management position will curtail further advancement.

9. When you start a new job, you have exceptional opportunities to lay the foundation for rapid advancement. Don't let these chances get away.

   • When beginning a new job, three often overlooked opportunities await you:

   1. You have a wide open field to learn more about the organization than anyone else. Your questions will be

expected and welcomed. Formal interviews will be appropriate as well. Knowing more about the organization than anyone else should be your goal. You can use your information in hundreds of ways later on to help you look good.

2. Your organizational contacts, made in the course of orientation and training, will be free from political bias because you are new. Therefore, this is a full and ripe time to learn your job well. Do your homework, execute your new tasks better because of your study, and soar to the top. Enjoy the distance you will have from office politics and maintain it as long as you can. You'll be respected for it.

3. Your interview landed you the job, so your superiors in the organization obviously think highly of you. This honeymoon period can last on and on if you carry over the tone of your entry into the first weeks and months of your new position. Don't get slack. Don't miss this golden opportunity.

10. Successful career women have an unfailing sense of humor.

   • Humor relieves stress, helps resolve conflict, motivates, energizes, and creates healthy chemical reactions in the body. Keep your humorous perspective.

11. You must believe absolutely in the benefits that customers, clients, patients, and others get from your product or service.

   • For you to apply fully your skills and energies — and accordingly advance your career — you have to know in your heart and head that you're providing something worthwhile. Your success is linked to your belief.

12. Passionately love yourself and your work.

- Real productivity is rooted in love. When you love yourself and your work, you'll find it easy to love other people, too. And love will come back to you automatically.